W9-ANU-365

MORRILL ELEMENTARY SCHOOL

3488000822275

PROPERTY OF
CHICAGO BOARD OF EDUCATION
DONALD L. MORRILL SCHOOL

394.10
PAR
c.l Paraiso, Aviva
Caribbean food and
drink

394.10
PAR
c.l
Paraiso Aviva

AUTHOR

Caribbean food and

TITLE

drink

DATE	BORROWER'S NAME	ROOM NUMBER
10/15/97	Teresa adair	307
1-6-03	Mrs Townsend	217
		215

PROPERTY OF
CHICAGO BOARD OF EDUCATION
DONALD L. MORRILL SCHOOL

CARIBBEAN
FOOD AND DRINK

Aviva Paraïso

PROPERTY OF
CHICAGO BOARD OF EDUCATION
DONALD L. MORRILL SCHOOL

The Bookwright Press
New York · 1989

FOOD AND DRINK

British Food and Drink
Caribbean Food and Drink
Chinese Food and Drink
French Food and Drink
German Food and Drink
Greek Food and Drink
Indian Food and Drink
Italian Food and Drink

Japanese Food and Drink
Jewish Food and Drink
Mexican Food and Drink
Middle Eastern Food and Drink
North American Food and Drink
Russian Food and Drink
Southeast Asian Food and Drink
Spanish Food and Drink

First published in the
United States in 1989 by
The Bookwright Press
387 Park Avenue South
New York, NY 10016

First published in 1988 by
Wayland (Publishers) Limited
61 Western Road, Hove
East Sussex BN3 1JD, England

© Copyright 1988 Wayland (Publishers) Limited

Typeset by DP Press, Sevenoaks
Printed in Italy by G. Canale & C.S.p.A., Turin

Cover *An outdoor market, Port-au-Prince, Haiti.*

Library of Congress Cataloging-in-Publication Data

Paraiso, Aviva.
  Caribbean food and drink/by Aviva Paraiso.
  p. cm.—(Food and drink)
  Bibliography: p.
  Includes index.
  Summary: Describes, in text and illustrations, the food
and beverages of the Caribbean in relation to its history,
geography, and culture. Also includes recipes for such
dishes as jug-jug and sweet cassava bread.
  ISBN 0–531–18231–2
  1. Cookery, Caribbean—juvenile literature. 2
Beverages—Caribbean Area—Juvenile literature. 3
Caribbean Area—Social life and customs—Juvenile
literature. [1. Cookery, Caribbean. 2. Caribbean Area—
Social life and customs.] I. Title.   II. Series.
TX716.A1P37 1989
394.1'09729—dc19
                                                 88–19369
                                                      CIP
                                                      AC

Contents

Introducing the Caribbean   4
The history of the Caribbean   7
Producing the food   11
Processing and distribution   16
Selling the food   18
Regional foods   21
Drinks   38
Carnival time!   41
Caribbean food abroad   43
Glossary   46
Further reading   47
Index   48

Introducing the Caribbean

The Caribbean is not just one country. It consists of more than thirty large islands and many smaller ones that form an arc from Florida in the United States to Venezuela in South America. The largest islands are Cuba, Jamaica, Hispaniola (which is made up of Haiti and the Dominican Republic) and Puerto Rico.

The islands are divided into three groups: the Bahamas, the Greater Antilles (Cuba, Jamaica, Puerto Rico and Haiti), and the Lesser Antilles (the Windward and Leeward Islands). Today, most of the islands are independent, but in order to investigate their food we shall be looking at them according to the countries that originally colonized them.

Most of the Caribbean islands are the summits of a submerged chain of volcanic mountains, so many of them are themselves mountainous.

This beautiful coastline near Port Antonio in Jamaica is typical of many Caribbean islands.

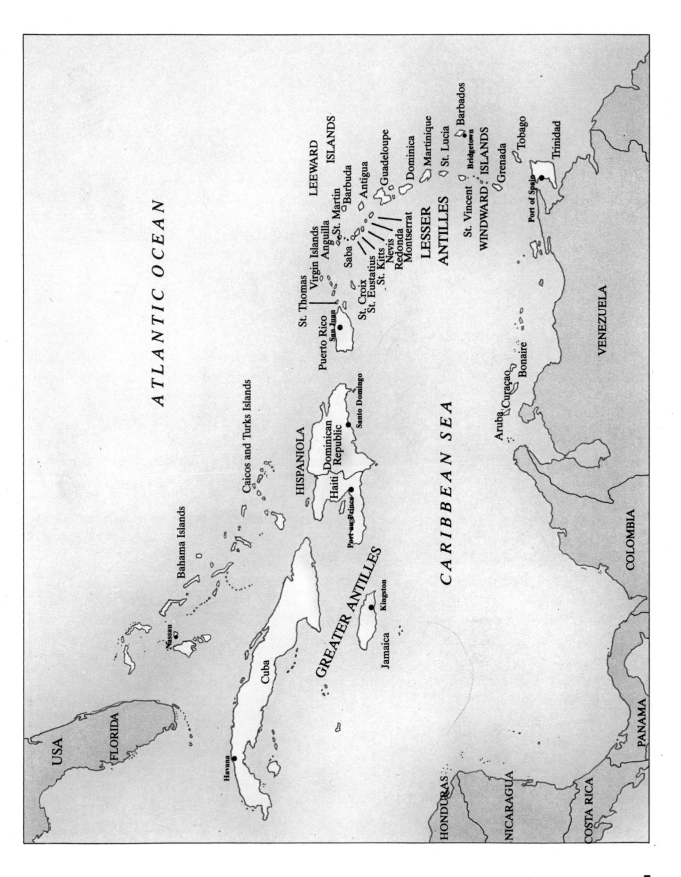

ATLANTIC OCEAN

USA
FLORIDA

Havana

Cuba

Bahama Islands

Nassau

Caicos and Turks Islands

GREATER ANTILLES

Jamaica

Kingston

HISPANIOLA

Haiti

Dominican Republic

Port-au-Prince

Santo Domingo

Puerto Rico

San Juan

St. Thomas

Virgin Islands

Anguilla

St. Martin

Saba

St. Croix

St. Eustatius

St. Kitts

Nevis

Redonda

Montserrat

Barbuda

Antigua

Guadeloupe

Dominica

Martinique

St. Lucia

St. Vincent

Bridgetown

Barbados

Grenada

Tobago

Trinidad

Port of Spain

LEEWARD ISLANDS

LESSER ANTILLES

WINDWARD ISLANDS

CARIBBEAN SEA

Aruba

Curaçao

Bonaire

VENEZUELA

COLOMBIA

PANAMA

COSTA RICA

NICARAGUA

HONDURAS

Some islands, such as the Bahamas, Barbados and Anguilla, are flatter and are made of coral limestone.

The total area of the islands is about 230,000 sq km (88,000 sq mi); the population is approximately 25 million. However, some islands are more densely populated than others. For example, there are a hundred times more people per square mile in Bermuda than there are in the Bahamas.

The islands are in the path of the northeasterly trade winds and the temperatures are generally hot, except high up in the mountains. The average temperature is 27°C (80°F). The maximum temperature

Violent storms, sometimes of hurricane force, sweep across the islands from September until November. This one is shown over the city of Havana in Cuba.

is 31°C (88°F) and the minimum 24°C (75°F). A short wet season begins in April and lasts between two and six weeks. This is followed by a dry season that lasts until July when the temperature rises. The hot season continues until September when there is a lot of rain and often violent storms. These are known as the "hurricane months." December marks the beginning of the long dry season, which continues until the spring.

The history of the Caribbean

The earliest inhabitants of the large islands of the Caribbean, such as Cuba, were the Siboneys, of whom little is known. They were followed by the Amerindian people and, later on, by the Arawaks. The Arawaks were a nomadic Mongoloid people who, over many hundreds of years, made their way northeast through Asia, into North America and South America. Some

This "jerked chicken" being barbecued in Jamaica shows the cooking technique brought to the islands by the Caribs.

made their way to the West Indies.

The Arawaks were hunters and fishermen. They occupied the Bahamas and some of the islands in the Greater Antilles. There were three tribes of Arawaks – the peaceful Lucayos in the Bahamas, the Tainos in Cuba, Jamaica and Haiti, and the more warlike Borinquens in Puerto Rico.

Later, the Carib people migrated from Brazil to the West Indies. They drove out the Arawaks by force and took possession of parts of Puerto Rico, Cuba and Hispaniola. The Caribs were unable to take Trinidad from the Arawaks, and their further expansion was stopped by the arrival of the Spaniards.

The Caribs and Arawaks had different diets. The Caribs were not such good farmers as the Arawaks, so they ate less of plant crops such as corn and *cassava*. However, they were better fishermen. As a result they ate more protein and were healthier and leaner than the Arawaks. The Caribs barbecued their meat and, therefore, they ate little fat.

The Caribs thought that eating turtle meat made people stupid, so they avoided it. They also believed that pork gave people small, beady eyes and that crab meat eaten before a sea voyage would bring on storms! Some of these beliefs,

Christopher Columbus presents an account of one of his four visits to the Caribbean to the King and Queen of Spain.

still affect what is eaten today.

Carib food was seasoned with pepper and pepper sauces such as *couii* and *taumalin*, but Caribs did not use salt. They also made a strong, alcoholic beer from *cassava*.

The first European known to have reached the Caribbean was the Italian Christopher Columbus, who undertook his voyage of discovery for the Queen of Spain.

On October 12, 1492, he first sighted the Bahamas and went on to explore many of the islands. He then established a base at Caricol Bay on Hispaniola. Columbus called the lands "las Yndias" as he thought he had reached the East. He did not change this to "las Yndias Occidentales" ("the West Indies") until 1502.

In 1493, Columbus returned and visited Montserrat, Redonda, Antigua, Nevis, St. Eustatius, St.

Kitts, Saba, Santa Cruz, Puerto Rico and the Virgin Islands. The community at Caricol Bay had disappeared when he reached Hispaniola. He massacred many of the Arawaks and sent others to Spain as slaves.

Columbus visited many of the remaining islands in his subsequent voyages of 1498 and 1502 and claimed the islands for Spain. The Arawaks were treated very badly by the Spanish and had almost

Although Britain made slave trading illegal in 1807, slaves continued to be used on the sugar plantations of the West Indies into the second half of the nineteenth century.

totally disappeared by the early seventeenth century.

In 1493, the Spanish introduced sugarcane to the rich, fertile soil of the West Indies. Previously, they had obtained their sugar from Cyprus. Slaves were needed to work on the sugar plantations, and a trade was started to bring them from West Africa by the Portuguese and, to a lesser extent, by the British and French.

In 1621, following a period of feuding between the Dutch and the Spanish in Europe, the Dutch West India Company was founded. A sea war followed, and the Dutch gained control of the seas around the Caribbean islands. The Dutch, English and Portuguese began their colonization of the West Indies by first establishing colonies, now known as Guyana, Surinam and French Guinea, on the coast of

These imported laborers from China are shown in Guadeloupe in 1860.

South America.

In 1626, the French and English jointly took the island of St. Kitts and massacred the Carib population. In 1629, the French were driven off the island by the Spanish but the English retained their control. Tobacco was established as a cash crop on the island of St. Kitts.

Nevis, Montserrat and Antigua became British colonies at the same time. Soon afterward, the English claimed Barbados as well. In 1670, Spain finally gave up Jamaica to the English.

Having been unsuccessful on St. Kitts, the French went on to establish colonies on Martinique and Guadeloupe.

In the 1630s, the Dutch, who were more interested in trading than in plantations, established colonies on St. Eustatius, Curaçao, Bonaire, Aruba, Saba and St. Martin.

At first, the main product of the Caribbean islands was tobacco but, by 1627, the crop being exported to Europe from the state of Virginia was so much bigger than that of the West Indies that the main agricultural interest turned to sugar production. Sugar required far more slaves to tend the plantations than had tobacco, so the Dutch began to bring 3,000 slaves a year from West Africa to the Caribbean.

The Dutch brought in huge numbers of slaves. In 1673 there were approximately 8,000 white people living in Jamaica and 10,000 black people; by 1741 these figures had increased to 10,000 and 100,000 respectively.

The slave trade to the West Indies was horrifying; in the eighteenth century the death rate on the journey from Africa was as high as 30 percent. It is estimated that as many as eleven million slaves were taken from West Africa in the period from 1515 to 1865. Britain eventually made trading in slaves illegal in 1807.

In addition to West Africans, other peoples have also moved to settle in the West Indies, though they were not forced there as slaves. These included Jews fleeing from the Spanish Inquisition in the sixteenth century and British leaving the United States after the War of Independence in the

The Rastafarian *cult represents one of the ways black people have tried to re-establish their identity after slavery.*

eighteenth century. Traders from Lebanon and Syria came in the nineteenth century. During the British rule of India, also in the nineteenth century, many Indians went to the West Indies as indentured laborers, most of them to Trinidad. At around the same time other indentured laborers arrived from China.

As can be guessed from this brief history, the peoples of the islands today are a mixture of many races. As a result, there is a wide range of cultural traditions, backgrounds and languages. The richness of this diversity is reflected in the food of the islands.

Producing the food

With the arrival of the Europeans, the Caribbean became an important agricultural area, producing food for export to Europe.

With the decline of the tobacco industry, sugar became the main export crop of the islands and remains very important today. The bulk of the sugar is produced in Cuba from where it is exported to the Soviet Union. Although new sugar refineries have been built on

In Cuba some sugarcane is still cut by hand.

Fish plays an important role in the West Indian diet. Much of the fishing on the islands is carried out using small boats such as this one in Barbados.

the islands, most of the refining is still carried out abroad. Many of the islands produce and export rum made from the fermented sugar.

Bananas are also an important export, the main crop coming from Martinique. Coffee, too, is an important export crop. The bulk of this comes from the Dominican Republic. Coffee is produced on a large scale only on the large mountainous islands, which provide suitable conditions for its growth. Other major Caribbean food exports include citrus fruits, cocoa and spices. Grenada grows nutmeg and ginger, and allspice comes from Jamaica. Flowers, and some tobacco, are also grown for export.

Market gardening is a major occupation on those islands that have sufficient supplies of fresh water to permit adequate irrigation. Many of the islanders grow fruit

This breadfruit has been cooked whole on an open fire.

and vegetables for themselves and keep some animals, such as chickens, pigs and goats. However, none of the islands are self-sufficient in food. Agriculture is made difficult by the steep slopes, poor soil and drought. Only 27 per-cent of the total land in the Caribbean is arable and only 14 per-cent is used for pasture.

Fish is important in the West Indian diet. However, fish caught in the area provides only about a quarter of the needs of the islands, and the remainder is imported. Shellfish are caught for export. Saltfish (dried and salted fish) is a major source of protein and does not require refrigeration.

The tropical climate means that a wide variety of fruits and vege-tables are produced on the islands, some of which are listed below. Many of these are now exported.

Ackee is the fruit of an evergreen tree from West Africa. It has a scarlet shell and shiny black seeds. The edible parts are small and yellow. It is used in the Jamaican dish saltfish and *ackee*.

Breadfruit is a large green fruit that comes from the South Pacific. When cooked, the yellowish-white flesh is a substitute for potato or rice.

Callaloo are the leaves of the *taro* plant or the Chinese spinach. They are used particularly in soup.

Cassava is a long, brown root vegetable with white flesh. It can be eaten as a starchy vegetable or made into *cassava* meal or flour. Tapioca and *Cassareep* are made from *cassava*. *Cassareep* is a liquid made from the *cassava* root, which is used as a meat preservative. The bitter *cassava* is poisonous until it is cooked.

Cho-cho, or *christophene*, is a squash, originally from Mexico. It has a prickly skin and tastes like zucchini when cooked.

Dasheen is the root of the *taro callaloo* and is cooked like a potato.

Green bananas are unripe bananas, which are cooked as a starchy vegetable.

Mango is an Asian fruit, which is green or red-skinned when ripe with yellow or orange flesh. It is eaten fresh or made into jam, ice cream, etc.

Pawpaw or *papaya*, when ripe, is yellow or orange. It can be 0.5 m (1.8 ft) in length. The unripe fruit is used as a vegetable, and when ripe it is eaten like melon.

Plantain is a large type of banana. Plaintains have to be cooked before eating. They are used in soups and as vegetables.

Soursop is a green fruit with spines. The pulp is used mostly for drinks and ice cream.

Sweet potato is a root vegetable with brown or pink skin and pink or white flesh. It can be cooked like a potato and is slightly sweet.

Yams are root vegetables that can weigh up to 5 kg (11 lb). The flesh is white or yellow and they are cooked like potatoes.

This Jamaican street market shows many of the fruits grown on the islands.

Processing and distribution

As we have already seen, two of the principal crops exported from the Caribbean are bananas and sugar. Islands such as St. Lucia rely almost entirely on their banana crop for trade with other countries.

Bananas spoil very rapidly and therefore have to be harvested quickly and carefully. It has only been possible to export large quantities of bananas since the development of refrigeration. As soon as they are ready for cutting, which is before they ripen, the large bunches of bananas are cut and taken to the packing station. Here they are checked for disease and are dipped and washed to help prevent their deterioration. They are broken into smaller "hands" and are carefully packed into boxes. The same day, these boxes are taken to the port and packed into the holds of refrigerated ships. When they arrive at their destination they are kept in refrigerated warehouses until they are required for sale and then they are carefully ripened.

Bananas grow all year around,

Great care has to be taken to make sure that the bananas are cut before they ripen.

Sugar is processed for rum and molasses at refineries such as this one in Jamaica.

but the plants have to be treated with great care. They are subject to disease, such as leaf spot, and have to be sprayed regularly. On some islands the government provides airplanes, which spray all the plantations regularly. Banana trees can also be seriously damaged by hurricanes.

Sugar is no longer the main export of the Caribbean, but it is still very important on some islands, such as Jamaica. The cane is ready for harvesting from late January until August. It has to be crushed as soon as possible after cutting and often it is loaded straight onto trains at the plantations and taken to the crushing plant. At crushing, the juice is removed from the cane. The cane fiber is called *bulgasse* and is used for composition board, animal feed and fuel.

Some of the juice obtained from the crushing of the cane is then fermented to make rum, another important export from the islands (see page 38). The remaining juice is boiled and strained. This produces a thick syrup and brown crystals. The syrup is stored and used for molasses, while most of the brown crystals are exported to be refined into sugar.

The docks are a vitally important part of life on the islands. None of the islands is totally self-sufficient for food and they rely on both local and international trade. In Jamaica, for example, bananas, sugar, rum, coffee and pimentos are exported, while flour and canned beef are both important food imports.

Selling the food

Trading and marketing are vital parts of life in the Caribbean. Many people now buy their food in supermarkets in the towns and in larger stores, which have been built on the outskirts to allow greater parking facilities.

On some islands, such as Jamaica, the government has set up a distribution and marketing system. Food is collected from the

Many people travel into the towns by bus to sell their produce.

These fruits and vegetables are for sale at an outdoor market in Port-au-Prince, Haiti.

farms and truck gardens on the island and is taken to the towns where it is sold in modern, hygienic markets.

On other islands, such as Haiti, people bring the food they have for sale to large, outdoor markets where shoppers can walk around and choose what they want to buy.

There is a famous fish market in Curaçao. The boats moor right

Street trading is an important way for many people to sell their surplus produce.

alongside the road and people buy their fish directly from them.

In addition to these organized markets, people can be found selling their surplus produce, such as fruit and vegetables, from stands outside their homes. Many people do their shopping this way.

20

Regional foods

The peoples of the Caribbean islands came from many parts of the world. They brought with them their languages, their religions and

Beans, such as these on sale in Jamaica, are a vital part of the islanders' diet.

Rice and peas

You will need:

1-lb can of red kidney beans or pigeon
  peas
1¼ cups of long grain rice
2½ cups of coconut milk
1 onion, finely chopped
1 hot red pepper, seeded and chopped
2 tablespoons of vegetable oil
1 teaspoon of thyme
salt and pepper to taste

What to do:

(1) Heat the oil in a frying pan and fry the
onion until it is golden brown. (2) Drain
the beans and place in a casserole with
all the other ingredients. (3) Cover and
cook over a very low heat for 20 to 30
minutes or until all the liquid is absorbed
by the rice.

their cultures. As part of their
culture they also brought recipes
and methods of food preparation.
The types of food now cooked and
eaten in the West Indies reflect the
wide variety of cultural influences
that have come to the islands.

Many of the islands passed from
one group of colonizers to another
and so, for example, Spanish
names such as *Sangre Grande* appear
on English speaking islands like
Trinidad. In addition to these
European languages, forms of
patois known as Creole are spoken
on many of the islands.

Although the islands can be
classified according to the countries

that first colonized them, it is not as easy to divide the islands into such clear groups when discussing their food. There are, as we shall see, certain types of food associated with the islands of each language group. However, the recipes have moved with the people and, therefore, a particular dish may appear on several different islands in slightly different forms. A good example of this is the famous Caribbean dish of rice and peas. The "peas" of the recipe are in fact beans, and the type of bean that is traditionally used can vary from island to island. This version of the dish, from Jamaica, (facing page) uses red kidney beans or *gunga* (pigeon) peas, but another type of cooked pulse could be substituted.

The Caribbean islands also have specialized cooking equipment. Homes in the cities may well be equipped in the same way as modern kitchens anywhere in the world, but there are older cooking techniques and equipment that are still used, especially in more rural areas. A "smokeless fireplace" is a large cooking stone built over the flue of a wood fire. It can still be found on some islands. The Caledonian stove is a wood- or coal-burning iron range with an oven and hot plates.

Coal pots made of iron or clay are still used, even in modern homes, for slow-cooking foods. In some areas, box ovens are still in use. These are wooden boxes lined with tin with a coal pot standing in the bottom and wire shelves on which to place the food.

The "Dutch pot" is an essential part of the Caribbean kitchen. A shallow, flat-bottomed pot, it can be placed on any type of stove or coal pot and is used for stewing, frying and pot-roasting. There is also a three-legged Dutch pot that is very deep and can stand directly over coals.

The *yabba* pot, made of glazed earthenware, can stand great heat. The *tawa*, or frying pan, shows the influence of Asian immigrants in its name. It is a flat iron griddle for baking bread and *roti*.

Part of the African heritage of the islands is found in the large mortars and pestles that are used for pounding plantain to make *foo-foo* (plantain balls or dumplings).

Grinding hot peppers, Jamaica.

23

Rice and peas cooked in a Dutch pot over a wood fire.

The Spanish-speaking islands

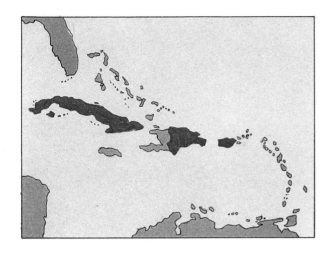

The Spanish colonizers brought many of their own foods and cooking methods with them to the Caribbean. Some of the fruits and vegetables they introduced, such as breadfruit, bananas, mangoes, coconuts and sugarcane, we associate today mainly with the Caribbean. The Spanish also introduced many pork dishes to the islands.

Escovitch (marinated cooked fish) is an example of Spanish cooking that has become part of Caribbean cuisine. *Escovitch* comes from the Spanish word *escabeche*, which refers to the method of pickling cooked fish in vinegar.

The rich *cocido de rinones* (a type of kidney stew) is another dish that

Below *Coconut, an important ingredient in many dishes, was introduced by the Spanish. Here it is being sold on the island of Haiti.*

reflects the Spanish influence on the cooking of these islands, as does *arroz con camerones*, a shrimp and rice dish that combines Spanish ingredients such as pimentos and olive oil.

A Cuban specialty is *maros y cristnos* – black beans and rice, a variation of rice and peas (see page 22). Black beans are used a lot in Cuban cooking and have an almost "meaty" taste.

Coconuts require a year to ripen; the annual yield per tree is about fifty.

A popular recipe on the island of St. Croix is *boija* (coconut corn bread). It gets its characteristic Caribbean taste from the combination of coconut and bananas.

The following recipe for *piononos* (stuffed rolled plantains) is from Puerto Rico and is traditionally served with rice and peas.

Piononos

You will need:

3 ripe plantains
1 lb of ground beef or pork
2 to 3 oz of chopped, boiled ham
3 eggs, beaten
1 onion, finely chopped
1 clove of garlic, chopped
2 tomatoes, seeded and chopped
½ green pepper, seeded and chopped
2 tablespoons of green olives, chopped
1 tablespoon of capers, chopped
½ teaspoon of oregano
vegetable oil
salt and pepper to taste

What to do:

(1) Peel the plantains and cut each into four slices. Heat the oil in a pan and fry them until golden. (2) Remove the plantains and, when they are cool, shape them into a circle and secure with a toothpick. Heat some more oil in the pan and add the beef. (3) When it is brown add the onion, garlic and peppers and cook until they are soft. Then add all the remaining ingredients except the eggs and cook until thick. Remove from pan. Heat more oil in the pan. (4) Dip plantain rings in beaten egg and fry quickly on both sides. Fill plantain rings with meat stuffing and serve.

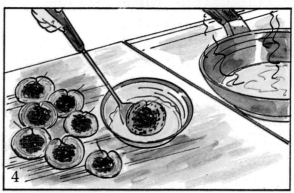

The French-speaking islands

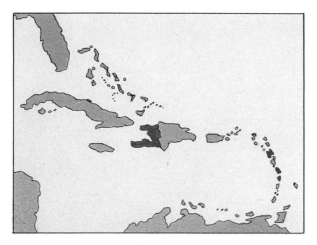

The French-speaking islands of the Caribbean are Guadeloupe, Martinique, Haiti, and part of St. Martin. Martinique and Guadeloupe are French *départements* and, as a result, have access to a wide variety of French foods. The French influence is to be seen everywhere on the islands, not least in the food people eat.

The traditional food of the French islands includes many fish and chicken dishes such as *fricasée de*

Below *This covered market is on the French-speaking island of Guadeloupe.*

Figues bananes fourrées

You will need:
3 large bananas
7 tablespoons of butter or margarine
a scant cup of confectioners sugar
2 tablespoons of raisins
3 tablespoons of lemon juice
3 tablespoons of unsalted peanuts, chopped
12 glacé cherries

What to do:
Peel the bananas and cut into halves both ways. Sprinkle them with lemon juice. Cream the butter and sugar together. (1) Cut a groove about ⅓ in deep into each banana and stuff with the butter cream. (2) Decorate with the peanuts, raisins and cherries. Place in refrigerator several hours before serving.

Safety note: Be careful when using sharp knives and always cut away from you.

poulet au coco (chicken in coconut milk – see page 30). Coconut milk is available from health food shops or specialty food shops. Alternatively, you can make your own by blending together the flesh and liquid of one coconut with 225 ml (1 cup) of boiling water and straining it through cheese cloth.

Fish plays an important part in the dishes of the French islands. A fish mousse made with red snapper is popular in Martinique as is court bouillon de poisson (fish cooked in a sauce of herbs and white wine). On the islands of Guadeloupe and Martinique, lime juice and garlic are the special ingredients that are added.

The island of Martinique grows more bananas than any of the other islands. The bananas grown here are ripened and sold in France. However, bananas are important to all the islands, and there are many recipes that include them. Figues bananes fourrées from Haiti is only one such recipe.

Fricasée de poulet au coco

You will need:
A small chicken, cut into quarters
1 large onion, finely chopped
1 lb of mushrooms, sliced
1 clove of garlic, chopped
3 tablespoons of vegetable oil
parsley
thyme
1 hot red pepper
1¼ cups of coconut milk

What to do:
Heat the oil in a frying pan and add the chicken quarters. (1) Fry them for about five minutes until they are golden brown on both sides. Remove the chicken and place in a casserole. (2) Fry the onion, garlic and mushrooms until tender. (3) Add all the ingredients to the casserole.

Cover and simmer for about 1 hour until the chicken is tender. Remove the pepper before serving. (4) Serve with rice.

The English-speaking islands

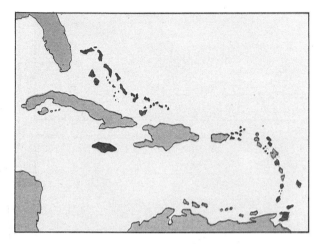

Many of the Caribbean islands are English speaking, and they have developed a tradition of cooking that still owes something to the influence of the British colonizers. As an example, one of the dishes that is traditionally eaten at Christmas in Barbados is *jug-jug* (see next page). This recipe is thought to have been developed as a substitute for haggis by the Scots who fled to Barbados after the Monmouth Rebellion in 1685.

Below *"Jerked pork" was probably introduced to Jamaica by the Caribs or Arawaks.*

Jug-jug

You will need:

3 to 4 oz of lean corned beef, cut into cubes

3 to 4 oz of lean pork, cut into cubes

1-lb can of pigeon peas or chick peas

2 onions, chopped

3 stalks of celery, chopped

3½ tablespoons of millet or couscous

1 tablespoon of parsley

1 teaspoon of thyme

3½ tablespoons of butter or margarine

2 scallions, chopped

What to do:

Cook the meats in a saucepan of water for 1 hour. (1) Strain the meat and add the peas. (2) Put the meat stock back in the saucepan and add the remaining ingredients except the butter. Cook gently for 15 minutes. (3) Chop or grind the meat and peas and add to the pan. Cook for 30 minutes. Stir in the butter and transfer to a serving dish. (4) Make into a smooth shape.

Perhaps the most famous traditional dish of Jamaica is salt-fish and *ackee*. It is usually served with fried plantain and rice and peas. Fish plays an important role in the recipes of the English-speaking islands as it does on all the islands. *Buljol*, a salt cod salad, is a favorite Sunday breakfast dish in Trinidad. Salt cod is also used in the Jamaican "stamp and go" (salt cod fritters). The name for these fritters is thought to have come from an old nautical term, but the name varies from island to island. Other popular varieties of food fish are flying fish and shark.

Jamaica is also famous for "jerked pork." This dish probably came from the Caribs and Arawaks and was later adopted by runaway slaves who seasoned a whole pig before roasting it over twigs. In Trinidad, a very special dish is *pasteles*, which are packets of cornmeal and meat wrapped in banana leaves. Sometimes they are eaten at breakfast, and they are eaten in large quantities over Christmas.

A popular lunchtime snack is beef patties. In Jamaica beef patties are the equivalent of the American hamburger.

The Dutch-speaking islands

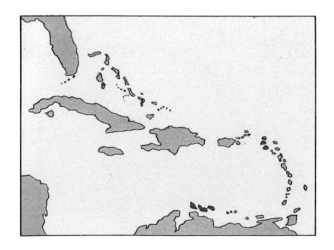

The Dutch islands of Curaçao, Aruba, Bonaire, Saba and St. Eustatius, like the other islands of the Caribbean, have developed a style of cooking based on local ingredients merged with African, Amerindian and European traditions. The Dutch gave to the islands one of its most interesting dishes, *keshy yena coe cabarone* (shrimp-filled Edam cheese – see next page).

Sopito is a fish and coconut soup, popular on the islands of Aruba and Curaçao. Made with salt meat and spices, it has an unusual flavor but is delicious. From the islands of Saba and St. Eustatius comes *funchi*, a type of cornmeal pudding that has a distinct African influence. Sometimes made with the addition of *okra*, it is found on several of the islands of the Caribbean and is called *coo coo* in Barbados.

Keshy yena coe cabarone

You will need:
A whole Edam cheese
1 lb of cooked, shelled shrimps
2 tablespoons of butter or margarine
1 lb of tomatoes, peeled and chopped
1 large onion, chopped
½ cup of breadcrumbs
2 eggs, beaten
3 tablespoons of raisins
2 tablespoons of sweet pickles
4 tablespoons of black olives, chopped
¼ teaspoon of cayenne pepper
Salt and pepper to taste

What to do:
Peel the wax off the cheese. (1) Cut off the top and hollow it out leaving a 2 cm (¾ in) shell. Soak the shell and lid in cold water for an hour. Grate ½ lb of the cheese. Heat the butter or margarine in a pan and cook the onion in it until tender. Add the tomatoes, salt, pepper and cayenne pepper and cook until thick. Remove from the heat. (2) Add the remaining ingredients including the grated cheese and fold gently together. (3) Dry the shell and stuff with the shrimp filling. Replace the lid and place the cheese in a casserole. Bake in the oven at 350°F for 30 minutes. (4) Remove from the oven and cut into slices.

Hindu foods

In addition to European-influenced foods, foods brought by people who have come to the islands from Africa and Asia over the years have added much to Caribbean cuisine.

When Asians came to the islands as indentured laborers, they brought the traditional meat and vegetable curries and breads of India with them. In particular this has influenced the cooking of Trinidad and has, of course, been adapted to the ingredients that are found on the islands.

The curry powder used varies from island to island. In Trinidad it is made from *massala*, a mixture of coriander seeds, anise seeds, cloves, cumin, fenugreek, peppercorns, mustard seed and turmeric. It is an important ingredient for many Trinidadian dishes, including *alu talkari*, a potato and mango curry popular in Trinidad.

Other Indian-inspired dishes to be found in the Caribbean are *roti* (see page 42), curried goat and *dal puri* (puréed split peas).

This breadfruit with curry sauce makes a quick take-out meal.

Pineapple drink

You will need:

The peelings and a little fruit of
   a pineapple
6 cups of boiling water
½ teaspoon of nutmeg
a few cloves

What to do:

(1) Place the peelings and cloves in a pot
and cover with boiling water. Cover and
leave for a day. (2) Strain and add the
nutmeg. Serve with ice.

Safety note: Take great care when
pouring the boiling water, or ask an
adult to do it for you.

There are numerous rumbased
drinks to be found on every island.

But with the wealth of fruit to
be found in the Caribbean, it is
not surprising that there are also
a great many fruit drinks to be
enjoyed as well. As you might
expect, considering the tropical
temperatures of the islands, many
of these drinks are cold and
refreshing.

Lemonade is always a favorite
drink. However, because the
lemons grown in the Caribbean are
usually small and hard, Caribbean
"lemonade" is more typically made
with limes.

Another very refreshing drink is
that made from the peelings of a
pineapple (see recipe). *Soursop*
drink is also popular.

Sorrel is a traditional Christmas
drink and is often made alcoholic by
the addition of rum. The sorrel used
is not the common herb but a
member of the hibiscus family
called rosella. Only the sorrel petals
are used.

Carnival time!

Whatever the occasion, the peoples of the Caribbean love to celebrate, but the biggest and most important celebration of the year is Carnival. Carnival occurs on many of the islands and takes place on the three days before Ash Wednesday as a preparation for Lent. During this time, people fill the streets, dancing, singing and wearing fabulous costumes as they "Jump Mas." The origins of Carnival come from Europe via South America. These traditions have been blended with other, possibly even older ones, from Africa.

As people dance in the streets all day they, of course, become very hungry. The food that they eat has to be simple as there is no chance to sit down. Stuffed *rotis* are very popular and many other Indian foods are also eaten at this time, such as *polouri* (split-pea fritters) and *kachouri*, which are made of chick-pea meal.

Chinese food is also popular at Carnival, and stands can be found selling pancake rolls and spare ribs.

Traditional Creole food is also sold and there are stands selling cakes and candies of coconut, sugar, honey and condensed milk.

These traditional Carnival costumes are from Haiti.

Roti

The Trinidadian *roti* is a close relative of the *chapati* of India. It can be served with a variety of fillings such as *alu talkari*.

You will need:
1¾ cups of all-purpose flour
3¾ teaspoons of baking powder
¼ teaspoon of salt
water
vegetable oil

What to do:
(1) Sift the dry ingredients together. Add water and mix it to a stiff dough. (2) Knead the dough thoroughly and shape into 5–6 balls. Cover with a cloth and allow to rise. (3) Roll out the balls on a floured board. Heat a griddle or heavy-based frying pan. Lightly oil the griddle or frying pan and place the *rotis* on it one at a time. (4) Brush them with oil and turn. Wrap them in a cloth to keep them warm.

Caribbean food abroad

For a long time Caribbean fruits, vegetables and recipes were largely unknown outside of the islands. Since the 1950s the large number of people emigrating from the Caribbean area has changed this. Communities established themselves in other countries and, of course, wanted to cook the food that they knew from their homeland. Therefore, markets, especially in large cities, have

The wide variety of Caribbean dishes has featured in magazines and on television programs in many parts of the world.

begun to cater to their West Indian populations. Bananas and coconuts have always appeared on the fruit stands of Europe, and ginger, nutmeg and allspice have been part of European cooking since the West Indies were first visited by the Spanish. But now all sorts of other fruits and vegetables previously unknown in Europe have begun to appear. At first, most Caribbean food such as *ackee* and breadfruit had to be bought in cans, but with improved refrigeration and travel, fresh fruits and vegetables from the

Markets abroad such as this one in London, England, have made Caribbean fruits and vegetables easily available.

Caribbean can now be purchased.

This has been followed by the appearance of Caribbean restaurants. Most serve food from many of the islands, and are becoming increasingly popular with both West Indians and other people.

West Indian food has also entered the snack food market and some fast food stands now sell dishes such as Jamaica patties.

The following chart shows the principal languages spoken on the different islands of the Caribbean although many people speak various patois versions of these languages. (The official language of St. Lucia is English. However, most of the population speak French patois.)

English	Bahamas Jamaica Turks Islands

	Leeward Islands:
	   Virgin Islands
	   St. Kitts, Nevis, Anguilla
	   Antigua, Barbuda, Redonda
	   Montserrat
	   Dominica

	Barbados

	Windward Islands:
	   St. Vincent
	   Grenada
	   St. Lucia

	Trinidad Tobago
Dutch	St. Martin (part) Curaçao Bonaire Aruba St. Eustatius Saba
French	Guadeloupe St. Martin (part) Haiti Martinique
Spanish	St. Thomas St. John St. Croix Puerto Rico Cuba Dominican Republic

Glossary

Amerindians Any member of the native races of North America.

Arawaks A group of Amerindians who reached the Caribbean about 2,000 years ago from South America.

Bauxite A type of clay compound from which aluminum can be extracted.

Bulgasse A waste product, produced during sugar production, which is used for fuel, animal feed and composition board.

Caribs A group of Amerindians from South America who traveled to the Caribbean after the Arawaks.

Cassava A tropical plant with edible starchy roots. The root or the starch extract from it is used in making bread and tapioca.

Chapati A type of thin, flat, unleavened bread from India.

Citrus fruits Fruits such as lemons, limes, oranges and grapefruits.

Creole A language developed in the West Indies and Gulf States, based on French or Spanish.

Département An administrative department of France. There are ninety on the French mainland and five *départements d'Outre-Mer* (overseas departments).

Griddle A flat metal surface or pan on which food is cooked.

Haggis A Scottish dish made of the heart, lungs and liver of a sheep, mixed with suet, oatmeal and onions and boiled in a sheep's stomach.

Indentured laborers Workers employed on binding contracts for a fixed period of time.

Irrigation Watering of land by digging artificial canals, etc.

Jamaica patties Small, flat pies containing meat or vegetables.

Jump Mas Dancing at the Carnival.

Molasses A thick syrup, which is a by-product of the manufacturing of sugar.

Mortar and pestle A bowl and pounder in which substances can be ground or pounded.

Nomads People who travel with their flocks or herds from one grazing site to another.

Patois A local dialect.

Pigeon peas The brown seeds of a tropical shrub (*Cajanus Indicus*).

Plantation An estate used for growing sugar, coffee, etc.

Pulses Edible seeds of certain leguminous plants, e.g. peas.

Siboneys Some of the earliest inhabitants of the Caribbean.

Spanish Inquisition A sixteenth-century trial in Spain held by the Roman Catholic Church during which non-Catholics were often tortured and put to death.

Tapioca Hard, white, starchy grains used most commonly for making puddings.

Further reading

The Caribbean: Issues in U.S. Relations, Raymond Carroll. Franklin Watts, 1984

The Fannie Farmer Junior Cookbook, Wilma L. Perkins. Little, Brown & Co., 1957

Follow the Sun: International Cooking for Young People, Mary Deming and Joyce Haddard. Sun Scope, 1982

Let's Look up Food from Many Lands, Beverly Birch. Silver Burdett & Ginn, 1985

Take a Trip to Cuba, Keith Lye. Franklin Watts, 1987

Take a Trip to the West Indies, Keith Lye. Franklin Watts, 1984

We Live in the Caribbean, John Griffiths. Bookwright Press, 1985

Picture acknowledgments

The publishers would like to thank the following for their permission to reproduce copyright pictures: Anthony Blake 20, 36; Mary Evans 8 (bottom), 9; Topham Picture Library 28, 43, 44; Wayland Picture Library 6, 8 (top), 12; ZEFA 15, 41. **All other photographs were taken by John Wright**. The maps on pages 5, 25, 28, 31 and 33 are by Malcolm Walker. All step-by-step recipe illustrations are by Juliette Nicholson.

Index

Africa 9, 10, 14, 23, 35, 36
African food 14, 33, 36–7
Amerindians 7, 33
Anguilla 6
Antigua 8, 9
Aruba 10, 33
Asia 7, 14, 23, 35

Bahamas 4, 6, 7, 8
Barbados 6, 9, 12, 31, 33, 38
Bermuda 6
Bonaire 10, 33
Britain 8, 9, 10

Caribbean Islands (see West Indies)
Caribs 7, 8, 9, 31, 33
China 9, 10
Chinese food 14, 41
Coffee 13, 17
Colonization 4, 22, 23, 31
Cuba 4, 6, 7, 11, 26, 38
Curaçao 10, 20, 33

Dominican Republic 4
Drinks 8, 14, 38–40
    rum 13, 17, 38

Fish 12, 14, 20, 25, 26, 28, 29, 33, 43
France 9, 28–9
Fruit 13–14, 19, 20, 25, 40, 44
    bananas 13, 14, 16–17, 25, 36, 44
    coconuts 25, 26, 33, 36, 39, 41, 44

Greater Antilles 4, 7

Grenada 13, 45
Guadeloupe 9, 28, 29
Guyana 9, 38

Haiti 4, 7, 19, 20, 25, 28, 29, 41
Havana 6, 38
Hispaniola 4, 7, 8

Indentured labor 9, 10, 35
India 10, 35
Indian food 10, 35

Jamaica 4, 7, 9, 10, 13, 14, 15, 17, 18, 21, 23, 33, 38

Leeward Islands 4
Lesser Antilles 4

Markets 15, 19, 43
Martinique 13, 28, 29
Meat 7, 17, 31, 33, 35
Montserrat 8, 9, 45

Nevis 8, 9

Puerto Rico 4, 7, 8, 26, 37, 38
Port Antonio 4
Portuguese 9

Rastafari 10
Recipes
    figues bananes fourrées 29
    fricasée de poulet au coco 30
    jug-jug 32
    keshy yena coe cabarone 34
    pineapple drink 40

piononos 27
rice and peas 22
roti 42
sweet *cassava* bread 37
Redonda 8, 45

Saba 8, 10, 33, 45
St. Croix 26, 45
St. Eustatius 8, 10, 33
St. Kitts 8, 9, 37, 45
St. Lucia 16
St. Martin 10, 28, 45
St. Vincent 45
Santa Cruz 8
Slave trade 8, 9, 10, 33, 36
South America 4, 7, 9, 14, 41
Soviet Union 11
Spain 7, 9, 10, 25
Spices 13, 36, 44
Sugar 9, 10, 11, 13

Tobacco 9, 10, 11, 13
Trinidad 7, 10, 22, 33, 35, 38

United States 4, 7, 10

Vegetables 19, 20, 25, 35, 43, 44
Virgin Islands 8

West Indies
    agriculture 11, 14, 16, 17
    climate 6, 14
    history 7, 10
    language 21, 22, 45
    population 6
Windward Islands 4